Once
Upon
a
Time
Called
Love

M Scotty Cogdell

Once Upon a Time
Called Love
M Scotty Cogdell

ISBN 13: 978-0615758329
ISBN 10: 061578320

mr. ma'at publishing

On the cover:
Charlene Casiano

This book is dedicated to everyone that love is in.

Disclaimer:
The author assumes no
responsibility if the
reader grows love as a
result of reading this
book.

Warning:
This book contains adult
language and themes.
(and no page numbers)

Table of Contents:

1. Infatuation

You don't know what just happened, but it just happened to you. A strange feeling floods your chest. Butterflies flutter around your stomach. You feel lightheaded, and none of your words seem to come out right. For some odd reason, none of this bothers you, and you feel FUCKING FANTASTIC! A great surge of energy keeps you awake at night with a smile on your face. When the sun rises, you can't wait to start your day. What the hell am I talking about?

Love. The most subjective word in any language. I am not attempting to define the word, or even influence your thoughts and feelings on love. This is my interpretation of a phenomena that you must discover and experience for yourself...

2. 'Round and Round We Go

Love will have your head spinning. Sometimes it feels as if we go in circles in the pursuit of love, or as a by product of it. There are seven main subtle energy centers in the body that spin at a high rate, called 'chakras' in Sanskrit, meaning 'wheel.' These chakras are also metaphorically called lotuses, being that they rise in the body like a lotus from muddy depths to blossom and kiss the sunshine. As our awareness progressively rises through the various chakras, so does the understanding of the natural refinement of love. Here is a brief outline of the chakras in ascending order:

I. Muladhara (moo-la-da-ra)
II. Svadhistana (swa-dee-sta-na)
III. Manipura (man-eh-poor-ah)
IV. Anahata (ahn-ah-ha-ta)
V. Vishuddhi (veh-shoo-dee)
VI. Ajna (ahj-nah)
VII. Sahasrara (sah-ha-sra-ra)

Let's climb up this ladder of love.

I. Muladhara: Ground Zero

Muladhara, the base, or 'root' chakra, is located in the physical body in the area of the perineum. Like the roots of a tree, love cannot reach towards the sun and grow if it is not rooted firmly in Mother Earth. Love at this level is the love that says, "I love you because you are the mother/father of my child(ren)." It deals with the survival of the species, i.e. procreation--let's make a baby. The most primal of urges. In some cultures, the concept is that sex is solely for the purpose of creating another life. It is the reason why cultures have pre-arranged marriages to ensure the most compatible union for healthy children in those particular societies. In the animal kingdom this process is known as natural selection. Evidence of this in nature is when you see male lions kill offspring that are not theirs, literally having the pick of the litter. Yet so many still wonder why men fight over pussy.

II. Svadhistana: Singularity

Svadhistana, the sex chakra, is located in the physical body in the area of the genitals. Every living being on this planet is a product of sexual energy. If this wasn't the case, you could not have been born (with the exception of an immaculate conception). Sexual energy is the energy of creation. In order for a flower to bloom, even a plant must use sexual energy. When an artist paints a picture, once again, that is sexual energy. Love at this chakra is equated with sex, primarily for pleasure. Yet equating love with the fulfillment of the urge for sexual pleasure is only sensory gratification, not to be confused with love. I liken this to a singularity, also known as a black hole, having a force so powerful that not even light can escape. If a person is not aware, sex can consume you like a black hole, where not even the light of your higher consciousness can escape.

III. Manipura: Inferno

Manipura, also known as the solar plexus, is located in the physical body in the area of the navel and abdomen. This is the power center. Here is where sex and love are used as control mechanisms to get what one wants. A prime example of this is when one partner in a relationship withholds sex or affection for material gain or until the other behaves in a manner selfishly desired. From this energy center is where the urge for sexual gratification is preyed upon in order to make a profit. Some of this is blatant, most of it is very subtle. Some of y'all know someone that if a man doesn't buy her a drink, pay a bill, or get her hair done, those panties definitely are not coming off. Most women won't engage in sexual activity until their material needs are met. For that very reason, most men go out of their way to get material things for a woman, or to make a woman feel comfortable. Why is this? Most men value sexual activity over material comfort, and literally fuck themselves out of house and home, while women fuck themselves into it. In women, the chakra system is anatomically synchronistic with her body. In men, the sexual organs reside lower than the root chakra (Muladhara), so the sex center (Svadhistana) is his ground zero. Men use sex as a weapon by treating women like property and having to be in charge. Big mistake. Manipura is the energy center where sex solely for gratification and dominance can consume your being and reduce you to ashes in the fiery furnace of the solar plexus. With awareness, Manipura is the chakra that offers you the opportunity to burn away the dross of egotism and sheer hedonistic lust, leaving nothing but the gold of pure love.

IV. Anahata: Crossroads

Anahata, the heart center, is located in the physical body in the area of the sternum, corresponding with the thymus gland. This is the center of transformation from selfishness to compassion, the crossroads of love. Here one can either rise or fall in love. Unconditional acceptance of others is one way to know if this is where you are expressing love from. It is the love of a mother for her child. In Anahata, love needs no reason, and one loves for the sake of love, seeking nothing in return. Devotion to another becomes possible, and one awakens to the fact that love is impossible without compassion.

V. Vishuddhi: Clarity

Vishuddhi is located in the physical body in the area of the throat, corresponding with the thyroid gland. This is the center of clarity, communication, and purification. The illusion of duality is transcended, as opposites are realized to not be two separate things, but different aspects of one. Here is where love goes with the natural flow of things. By letting things happen as they are supposed to, harmony with all in one's environment is ensured. Feelings and thoughts of love are expressed freely, with a definite degree of certainty, since the truth needs no alibi. Love is shared from this center without apology, as perceived boundaries disappear, such as religious or political segregation. The world has no borders when love is manifested at this level, as one's being begins to blend with all of existence.

VI. Ajna: Discernment

Ajna, or the third eye, is located
in the area of the forehead
between the eyebrows,
corresponding with the pineal
gland. This is the center of
awareness and discernment. Love
at this spiritual center is what
some would call a religious
experience. Great intuition is
automatic, and you see things for
what they really are. Love
manifesting from this center is
completely sincere, and unable to
be taken for a fool. An innate
intelligence arises that precludes
thought, and all pretenses are
dropped, as a great knowingness
arises. It is when you look into
the eyes of your beloved and
neither physical contact or words
are needed in order for two to
become as one.

VII. Sahasrara: The Big Bang

Sahasrara, the crown chakra, also known as the 'Thousand Petaled Lotus,' is located in the physical body at the top of the head. This is the manifestation of Divine Love. Here is where love from the cosmos enters and animates our being(s) as a fundamental particle, an orgasm of existence, shared with the infinite womb of the void. Love exists here whether we are aware of it or not. Expressed mathematically as $1/137$, love realizes its boundless potential. It is not the love for God, or the love of God.
Love is God; God is Love.

3. iLove U

Afrikaans - Ek is lief vir jou
Albanian - Te dua
Amharic - Afekrishalehou
Arabic - Behebik
Armenian - Yes kez wiremen
Basque - Maite zaitut
Bengali - Ami tomake bahlobashi
Bosnian - Volim te
Bulgarian - Obicham te
Cantonese - Ngo oiy ney a
Catalan - T'estimo
Cheyenne - Ne mohotatse
Chichewa - Ndimakukonda
Creole - Mi aime jou
Croation - Volim te
Czech - Miluji te
Danish - Jeg elsker dig
Dutch - Ik hou van jou
English - I love you
Esperanto - Mi amas vin
Estonian - Ma armastan sind
Ethiopian - Afgreki
Farsi - Doset daram
Filipino - Mahal kita
Finnish - Mina rakastan sinua
French - Je t'aime
Frisian - Ik hald fan dei
Galician - Querote
German - ich liebe dich

Greek - S'agapau
Gujarati - Hoo thunay prem
karoo choo
Hawaiian - Aloha wau ia oi
Hebrew - Ani ohev otah
Ani ohev et otha
Hindi - Hum tumhe pyar karte
hae
Hmong - Kuv hlub koj
Hungarian - Szaeretlek
Icelandic - Eg elska thig
Indonesian - Saya cinta padamu
Irish - T'a gr'a agam dhuit
Italian - Ti amo
Japanese - Kimi o ai shiteru
Korean - Dangsinul saran ghee yo
Latin - Te amo
Latvian - Es tevi milu
Lithuanian - As tave myliu
Malaysian - Saya cintamu
Mandarin - Wo ai ni
Norwegian - Jeg elsker deg
Polish - Kocham ciebie
Portuguese - Eu te amo
Romanian - Te iubesc
Russian - Ya tyebya lyublyu
Sanskrit - Twayi snihyaami
Serbian - Volim te
Sesotho - Kiyahurata
Slovenian - Ljubim te
Spanish - Te amo

Swahili - Nakupenda
Swedish - Jag alskar dig
Tagalog - Mahal kita
Thai - Phom rug khun
Chan rug khun
Ukranian - Ya tebe kokhayu
Urdu - Main tumse megabit karta
hoon
Vietnamese - Anh yeu em
Em yeu an
Welsh - Rwy'n dy garu di
Yiddish - Kh'hob dikh lib
Zulu - Ngiyakuthanda

4. Unconditional

Unconditional love. What's that? The concept of love or what is accepted as love has been conditioned by society and media. For example, in Western society, the mind of the general population has been conditioned that the way a man is supposed to show his love for a woman is to buy her diamond ring. This is a relatively new concept based upon a much older tradition. Before diamond rings were popular and accepted as the norm, a dowry was usually given to the family of the bride to show the groom's worthiness, and also to compensate the bride's family for the loss of the wealth of their human resource from their communal labor pool. All of these things are done because of love, or so we are led to believe, hence the reason I say that most people's concept of love is conditioned.

Turn on the radio, and what are the songs your hear?

'Oooh, baby, I have to have you.'

'Baby I miss you.'

' I love you so much, I can't live without you.'

'I was fooled into loving you.'

'Why did it end?'

'When will I find love?'

'You don't know it yet, but I love you.'

'I will be yours forever.'

'Please don't leave.'

'I'll fuck you like no other.'

Et cetera

Et cetera

Your ass is being conditioned on how and what to feel.

So now you decide to turn on the television, and what do you see? Sitcoms full of sexual tension, played in primetime. Commercials for male enhancement products. Sex for sale, disguised as love.

It doesn't stop here. Open your favorite magazine. How many articles are discussing anything pertaining to the opposite sex? Either a picture of an attractive person is in most of the advertisements, or a question is being posed on how to make oneself more attractive, usually by learning how to exploit sexuality. All in the pursuit of, and in the name of love. Conditioned.

Unconditional love? Where do we begin? What do we start with? Clarity. The ability to see things as they really are. Acceptance. Not forcing conditions on what is. Discernment. Knowing when to hold on, and when to let go.

Instructions for love: wash, rinse, repeat, no conditioner necessary.

5. Unrequited

One of the beautiful things about love is that it can be given without the expectation of being returned, even though that's not how the majority of our society operates. We live in a 'what's in it for me?,' and an, 'I did all this for you, so now you owe me,' day and age. It doesn't have to be this way. Love grows itself when given freely, for love is its own reward. It is actually possible to be intoxicated with love, yet it is impossible to overdose. Love will have you thinking thoughts like: "The flowers taste prettier when looked at through honey." Crazy, right? It doesn't seem crazy when you're in love. Love will even make some people write poetry. Guess what? Here goes some poetry:

Selflessness:
selfishness doesn't hurt
only selflessness does
willingness
to accept reality
as it is
and courage enough
to do nothing
because that's all
one can do
anyway
time heals all wounds
only if one isn't afraid
to feel pain
and keep moving on
staying still
ending the beginning
while beginning the end
love only exists
right now

Ebb and Flow:
the silence of our spirits
causes waves when we whisper
the sound of our heartbeats
same as the sound on the beach
feeling each other
the sand under our feet
flowing with the full moon
until the tide ebbs again

Unconditionally:
infinite possibilities
are to be encountered
U exponentiate
the availability of experience
to be shared
because you're willing to accept
me
for who I am
the person U see
when U look in the mirror
we didn't ask to be
in possession of
this compatibility
recognition
means let's find bliss
and not resist
the persistent
need for life
to be itself
oneself
of U & me
love

Mirror Image:
our auras intermingle
dissolving into one
refreshing what retreated
the thing we thought
to be deceased
the spirit of Love
am i your reflection?
or are U mine?
looking into
the image of myself
something I see
nowhere else

Traveling to Bliss:
may I enter your temple
and experience the universe
traveling past distant galaxies
exploring inside of me
sitting still on my lap
me finding God
while being inside of U?
let's make this journey together
as each other's starship
living free
locked safely in each other's arms
learning the secret of the Sphinx
thinking nothing
feeling everything
defining intimacy
balancing polarities
offering myself on your altar
of femininity

Daybreak:
i watch the sunrise
as an erection
in the night sky
warming dark thighs
in between
day and night
shining a light
so warm and bright
the moon closes her eyes
while clouds begin to cry
the Earth shakes in anticipation
awaiting his return
as he embraces her
making the world turn
desires of old
burning away
love is how to live
day by day

Inhalation:
one day my soul shattered
the fragments of my mind
lost somewhere in time
my heart not understanding
the love everyone has or had for
me
then intuition said
U have one more chance
to let your spirit dance
and i listened
now the sun glistens
from the light i shine
finding myself inside myself
finally breathing my first breath

Finality:

the say love conquers all things
can it beat a broken heart?
first round knockout
heartache seemingly undefeated
down but not out another love
TKO
when i just wanted to go
for the win
but i lost your heart
a long time ago
now your absence is starting to
show
it seems i can't grow
too close to another
since thoughts of U pillage and
plunder
any chance of learning another
i love U still so much
but we're too far out of touch
where did our separation really
begin?
when will it end?
i don't know
but we're not together now
so i can't pretend
that I'm hurting
and U seem to
not give a shit
it is truly over

Holding Hands:
i just couldn't resist
to kiss your beautiful shoulder
oh so bare
one of our intimate moments
oh so rare
please excuse me
i didn't intend to offend
yet the sweet taste
lingers on my lips,
my hands where shaped by your
hips
which shouldn't be afraid
of my touch so much
let me reach
beyond our minds
so we can find each other
our true selves
standing naked in the sun
laying nude under the moon
soon to see eternity
embracing the fragility of life
love's tough enough to take care
of itself
so why don't we trust it enough
to take care of us?

In Between (Relationships):
i can still feel
the pulse of your heartbeat
as i savor the sweetness
of your kiss upon my lips
love given so freely
taking me by surprise
my soul frozen
by the reflection in your eyes
U light my fire
destroy all desires
for anything else
because nothing is left
i will answer
anytime U call my name
during joyous lovemaking
or first and last labor pains
insanity in these times
realizing it's the same calamity
as love
what's the use?
arguments and emotional bruises
too many fuck you's
please kiss me again

Amnesia:
play a song of silence
for love
place a wreath
under its bed sheets
fire a semi-automatic
21 gun salute
falling in love
is stupid
it's safer
jumping from an airplane
with no parachute
oops
it happened again
bending the rules
doing something
i said i wouldn't do again
how did it begin
when will it end?
euphoria arguments loneliness
what kind of cycle is this?
quenching my thirst
then getting me pissed
i miss U
and still trying to forget

No Words:
the way U look at me
when U don't say a word
let's me know
every word was heard
unspoken communication
thoughts salivating
feelings marinating
experiencing the intimacy
of U being real with me
i will do my best
to repay the favor
savoring every moment
that U are with me
i have no idea
what U are thinking
i believe enough
in freedom
that it might not
be about me
yet the reality
of our brief
eye contact
lets me know
in 3 −2 −1
we have made
contact
the reason
that everything happens

Spirituality Becoming:
i can still smell U
on me
and feel me
inside of U
the taste of your kiss
remains on my lips
i wish
it couldn't wash off
yet content
that the experience
recreates itself
with a simple thought
of the mind
and the beat of our hearts
we are one

Please:
can U be
the Divine Mother
and sing a lullaby
for all?
comforting
the humanity in me
as my ear rests
on your Bosom
listening to your heartbeat
only U can
ease the pain
show a man
how to breathe again
and trust U
after his spirit
has been broken
please hold my hand
though i'm scared to ask
permission
to love U

Nothing Lasts Forever:
the only thing
i fear
at this time
is that
i'm not scared
to let U go
if it means
U will be free
if U feel
not trapped in bondage
from me
physically, mentally, or spiritually
then feel free
to stay
where U will always be
in my heart
if not
i must keep going
for i cannot stop
on my path
just glad
U are willing
to walk with me
this far

Equality:
two becoming one
how much closer
could we be
i don't know
as we grow together
infinitely
our mature relationship
still in infancy
older than eternity
the sensitivity
of our intimacy
reality
recognizing love
when U look at me
i do believe
God smiles
every time we meet
answering prayers
allowing us to hold on
to each other as we sleep
wondering
is it all a dream
until i wake up and realize
U are still here with me

Breathe:
U remind me
so much of myself
it is impossible
to forget
who i am
U don't have to
remember me
i know whose eyes
in the mirror
that U see
i don't believe
us sharing God's Love
is impossible
to achieve
already a reality
inhale
exhale
becoming one
waking up together
breathe

Exhale:
i thank U
the only way I know how
opening my heart to humanity
now listening to inner sensitivity
Namaste
to yours my soul bows
no regrets
since the phoenix rises
after my ashes burn out
searching for immortality
finding it within
love never going without
waking up to awareness
living in the now

Lasting Moments:
life with U
is so easy to me
i'm not used to it
not afraid
just wondering how
it could be
so simple
so beautiful
are U a reflection?
or shining your light
on me?
i have to thank U
for waking up my inner
sensitivity
realizing every moment together
may be the last
i would like U in my future
though selfishly
and appreciate our past infinitely
realizing right now
is all we'll ever have

Transitions:
i wish i could do the things
i wish i could do for U
at least as small
tokens of appreciation
for what you've done for me
teaching me and i learn
what it means to be
loved unconditionally
i can't promise
and won't ask
for eternity
i worship your divinity
if U ain't feelin' me
i thank U always
for once loving me

Escape from Samsara:

the Love that exists between U &
me
is as the bumblebee and the tree
one grows from a seed and from
its flowers
the other comes to be
drinking her precious nectar
naturally pollinating species and
creating honey
an eternal bond
where fondness holds hands
cremated ashes are mixed
together
dissolving into the ocean of
eternity
reborn one day into sand
ashes to ashes and dust to dust
Tantra evolving Love from lust
the breath of life binding husband
and wife
to freedom enough to realize
what's inside all of us
when we wake up from the dream
U are what U believe
which is nothing
the most beautiful thing
so what is it truly
to be a human being living with
clarity?

Om Mani Padme Hum:
O Goddess
i offer myself on your altar
all that is me
only if she
allows me to enter
the temple
as our energies blend
rising from centers of
regeneration
to in-between our temples
ascending beyond Bindu
so i may honorably worship U
and recognize the divinity
actualizing inside myself
honestly taking a step
removing separation
moving into acceptance
of the togetherness
of being alone
with each and every breath
O Goddess
please breathe life into me

Let It Go:
don't let Love
fuck U up
trapped in what U think it is
because it is
and it isn't
at the same time
see what i mean?
don't waste time
trying to figure it out
since when U do
it changes once again
into something new
itself

Rebirth:
nothing lasts forever
not even the rising sun
the full moon
is always made new again
the seasons of life
flow like a current
and ebb like the tide
stolen moments in between
Love pays the price
nothing is free
or so it seems
babies don't ask to be born
so no one has to ask
to die
live long enough
the circle will complete itself
enjoy every breath
no matter what it brings
one day
it will all be over
or all over
again.

About the author:

Scotty is truly an individual with his own monarchy. I have witnessed him engaging in his craft of writing and martial arts physically, surrender himself mentally to his ideas...and eventually find himself spiritually through love of self and forging forward.
- by A. Joy
(the beautiful woman whose love gave me the gift of fatherhood...)

"The path is made by walking"
-African Proverb

also by the author:

between Zen and Tao